CW01095809

That Place

poems by

Ana Martínez Orizondo

Finishing Line Press
Georgetown, Kentucky

That Place

ACKNOWLEDGMENTS

A delay in your routine, previously published in *Beyond Words Literary
Magazine*
The Snake and the Eagle finalist for the 2022/23 Sandy Crimmins National
Poetry Prize
I am transparent, revised, original published in *From Whispers to Roars*
Earth-root, previously published in *Newtown Literary*
Convergence III honorable mention haiku contest winner, previously
published in the *Dreamers Creative Writing Magazine*
Respira, previously published in *The Blue Mountain Review*

Publisher: Leah Huete de Maines
Editor: Christen Kincaid
Cover Art: Ana Martinez Orizondo, *A place called home*
Author Photo: Jackie Taylor
Cover Design: Elizabeth Maines McCleavy

Order online: www.finishinglinepress.com
also available on amazon.com

Author inquiries and mail orders:
Finishing Line Press
PO Box 1626
Georgetown, Kentucky 40324
USA

Contents

a delay in your routine

as you gather the leaves
and trim the hedges,
look up at the sky

as you undo the sheets
and fold the linens,
stop and stay still

as you count the wrinkles
and powder your nose,
question the image, touch the glass

as you butter the toast
and pour the tea,
remember the joke, chuckle

as you plant the basil,
sink your fingers in the soil,
see how far they can go

I am transparent

I woke up tattooed by a fairytale
not of rabbit holes and white horses
or talking mirrors and hunchback saviors
but of cellular Oneness and grace.
I woke up barefoot in heaven
tingled by cold grass
awakened by the aroma of fertility
guayava and mamoncillo
as they procreated the earth
moved to the rhythm of son
raw and ripe
flexed the spine of Time
birthed a placenta of ocean.

Transparency is my name
I walk among you
I exist in children's laughter
bark and root of purpose and meaning.
I exist when you close your eyes
and float in forgiveness.
I exist where you rarely seek
it would take courage to find me.

I am transparent
yet
if you held out your hand
you would find me.

Respira

A breeze twirled around me, as if a fan hung from the sky.
I was six, back in Santa Clara, Cuba
a hot, foggy day when I could not breathe.
Abejas y mariposas jugando
descalza.

Two guitars strummed, hers and Mami's, July, 1971
the tall windows in the house spread wide
like their songs, la paloma blanca cruzando el azul.

Cool and shady inside, el aire se escapaba.
Mi boca se abría y solo salía un sonido,
como el canto de las ballenas.
¿Dónde estás Mami?

Beyond de gold-colored knob
she and Mami faced each other on the lace-covered bed.
La luz, backlight
blurry black and white dancing
silhouettes in-and-out, in and out
to an imaginary bolero.

I closed the door and retreated.
Mi cuerpo pequeño cayo sin aire sobre la loza fría.
Awakening the mothers from their secret spell.

Cuatro palmas calientes rezaron en mi espalda.
"Dios ayúdala" said she,
"Virgencita por favor ayúdala…
respira mi hija. Respira."

Earth-root

I searched along the rim of long hours
waiting pacientemente for a sign
contemplating, assimilating, once upon a time.

How many wasted words it took
palabras, y páginas
pages and pages of nothing
to end where I began
en el mismo principio
the place I will return
lugar del regreso.

A journey I mistook for land
(donde yo no pertenezco)
mistook for gold y el llamado "American Dream" que no es un sueño
mistook for the love I could not own, keep or brand cariño.

Al fin un día I simply stopped. I gave up the anguish
las congas y tambores, y pare de bailar.
I went back inside where it's dark and tongues are silenced
where borders and geographies are imaginary
and there, from my bare feet
una palma real sprouted my name
Earth-root, madre of all things
que no se nombran.

My third mother

While I held my mother's hand by the merengue offerings
puffing on a cigar, in her white laced dress en la fiesta de Santa
Barbara
la mulata said I was hija de Ochún.

Placed in a corner, five floors up from a street in Queens,
Mami looked down into my eleven ocean eyes, and uttered the word
Ochún
tightening her grip around my hand.

Mami lived in-between, between América
and a sleepless serenade called Cuba,
between her love for another woman and a roleplay of what will
others think
el que dirán, el que dirán, sung like a chorus.
I was scared because she was scared,
She was always scared
and fear
is borderless.

In-between those two dark walls,
la clave del guanguancó ran up my chubby torso
my feet wanting to be bare touching earth
and the curiosity over my - new - third – mother,
like a third eye on my forehead.

Vamonos antes del Bembé, the mounting of the orishas
and a door closed behind me.
The only contorted tongue and body was my own.
Keeping my mouth shut,
while speaking *inglés* inside my box of secrets.

Not only did I have two mothers, now I had a third.
Her name was Ochún and she liked the color yellow.

Hymn

Rose petal floating, red skin
hymn on my wide palm
inside the ocean, womb deep.

The snake and the eagle

Brother
why did you wait so long to tell me about the snake?
How was I to know that snakes crawl through pipes and linoleum
up bunkbeds in West New York, New Jersey?

How was I to imagine that a snake lullabies with its tongue
to numb a little boys' legs?
That it is so quiet, Mami never got up to kill it.
Don't snakes make a hissing sound
or is it a shhhh to calm their victim?

Why did you wait fifty years?
Mami had only talked of the sea monster in the bathtub
the one that appeared daily at four p.m. while I watched another
Gidget movie.
How does a J&B drinker with bony hairy ankles, writhe?

I was busy licking vanilla ice cream sandwiches,
blowing bubbles with double-mint gum
running up and down escalators,
things we dreamed about
when we chased dragonflies.

II

Brother
I have never seen your body
propel forward, as if to strike her.
Chest lifted while holding the last drops
of your second bottle.
Mami's breathing,
like the knife she held
against the white plate, clicking.
She did not open her mouth.

Please let her speak.

On that bench, where the three of us
had come together
to break bread with our fingers
and dip in olive oil,
wood became fire.
You could not stop.
This was your house,
this was your story,
this was your moment,
to attack.

I knew you were an eagle.
You once told me so.
It is my spirit animal, you said.
We pounce on our prey
from above, and constrict their air supply.
But I had never seen
so much of our father in you
pouring, spilling
the ten-year-old self
like red wine on white linen.

III

Brother
forgiveness
is not what eagles do.
No te nace.
Mother, Mami, Mom was crushed
you triumphed in your home
turf with claws
wrapped in words in the woods.

There is nothing.
Nada, left.
But an eighty-five-year-old
woman, called madre,
breathing out of a coiled tube
in your sundeck
saying, yo no sabía.
Looking down at the fresh cut tomatoes
from your garden,
clutching the embroidered cloth napkin
you bought in St. Tropez.
I didn't know, mi hijo.
I didn't know.
Yo no sabía.

Your tongue

Are you still down
south
between
II

yellow lines, empty
holding on, highways
Harley and lies?

I
sometimes
think of your
tongue.

Escondite

Inside a womb of bricks
by the construction site
after the multi-colored piñata
exploded,
I hid.

Escondite.

Birthday white
cotton-dress,
the one with the painted Pinocchio,
still white, felt
light under the blinding heat.

He jumps in, thick
black hair, wavy
boyish torso, naked
hands, sweaty chains
around my small arms
back shoved, pressed
against the prickly grey cement
in no-one's land

and kisses me.

Yellow ribbon

Under my pillow, Elvis
on a postcard, a tooth
inside a small plastic bag
a red ribbon.

Next to my single bed
ten dolls, a bicycle
four padlocks
on the front door.

Tomorrow I will win
first place in vocabulary.
A purple ribbon
with gold letters.
My English is excellent,
Ms. Natoli said.

Yesterday, the girl
with a yellow ribbon
stepped on my foot
black on blue.
Laughed on the stairwell.

I said *tenis*. Sneaker
you idiot.

That place

She sits to hear the seagull snatch
and measure her prey.
See the sailor, fisherman
and the floating dock,
catch shadows
against the yellow and purple
foggy full moon.
She clocks the crawl of night
where ghosts seek
and lover's cry.
And listens to the drowned
calls for home, that place.
Never quite made it there.

Miami

Highways aren't veins
palms search for sky, erect
doubtful sway
blurry photographs, burnt.

I forgot about you.

Deleted the map, here
even my weddings
shoved under the sand
coconuts, platano
jasmin de noche.

Now, you grow on me
like Spanish moss.

See me

Break the glass window!
Don't growl!
Shard the ceiling,
ink the photographs, sting
squish the earth
with a blow.

When you are done
will you

pick up the broken
re-orient the roots
find the multi-colored light
crackling
here

see me?

An opening

I

Years spent on the hammock
of your eyelids,
sitting pa-tien-tly.
Palms locked in prayer
hoping
river water washes
unrequited words
wondering when will
your almond eyes
look back at mine
once again
sweetly?

II

The nearness
of death,
an opening.

III

Tender your tired eyes, yet
still stuck in the clingy
chaos of want
not things,
but the inescapable trap
of that
which has no form.

IV

I am free
of you
and that.

The enigma of tenderness

I don't know what to do
with your hand on my cheek
that region below the eyes
above the jawline
between the nose and the ear
Michelangelo knows it well
not I
I cannot measure tenderness
crimson or indigo
a shadow can't sing.
How do I paint a song?

Asking for forgiveness

F
  a
    l
      l into the w
             e
           l
               l of my h p
                     i

and caress me in my sleep.

Centers of life and death in a place called home

A shrine
of her dead dog
in the bedroom, fake
fireplace, lights
the living.
Paper plates
are easier, she says.
No need to clean
ovens that don't work.

She brings me the elegy,
as if serving café,
written and laminated
on a four by six card
and points to
the floor by the rocking chair,
her dead dog's favorite spot.

A cazuela
cooks for me, she adds.
I can turn on
the candles
with a remote.

Estoy bendecida.

Sustainability

There is an herb
in your garden

it grows

from your fingers
to my mouth

It is said
to cure the spirit
absorb our tears
return them inside
earth

if not tended
ice it becomes
roots,
poison

I have yet to taste.

Convergence III

Yesterday's full moon,
wet from uncensored kisses,
dew of morning song.

Silent prayers

Silence breathes
the day before the Dragon Moon
Slow is time
in the village of Abiquiú
Silence
what cowboys stole from each other
Silent
the red rock
ripple on the mountain

I am but gravel
dinosaur bone
under the horse's hoof
dry mud
on the wrinkled bark

one moon is not enough
tres lunas shine
on tips of crosses, cliffs
of death and sacrifice

hear my prayers.

Jasmine and sage

I want to conquer your skin
like a scent
recognize you in darkness
inhale the sweat of moonlight
between ancient books, shaman's memory
see the sculpted pillow
molded dawn,
face of sand and waves

yet then I
regress
vacillate between
jasmine   and   sage

impossible to bottle
never a territory
numinous
a talisman for the before
being human

yet then I

The in-between

I rest my elbows
on the thin wood slab
do I push
the window open
let the wind billow

or remain
elongate the time of butterflies
somewhat enjoying
the when of rainbows?

What was the distance
between your hand and mine
at the dinner table?

Still as dead bones
fingers breathing each other alive.
Would my wrist have a pulse
without yours?

Never have I been so grounded
in turmoil

wanting
to be Banyon Tree
roots beyond self
envelop you
like octopus its prey

six inches of space
is enough
to never meet.

Inside the chasm of pressed hips

bones tell-not-narratives
stories utter-not-language
here
desire plays on violin curves
and cello strings
wide and open,
bandoneons echo
in tenor tunnels.
In this place
my name, I am
apple
and you your name,
bite
the solemn torrent
of my cream-filled marrow.

The Return

I have a theory
a knowledge from far away

when we die
we become
trees

grotesque
magnificent
full
naked
contorted
embraceable
dismembered
fertile

alive.

I want to fall into you

no longer am I
soft and malleable
watery

full of rocks
are my legs
hands rest dry
beatless
cemented heart.

I no longer fall in.

tiny, an elegy

tiny you were
versed on vodka, scripture
gin on kitchen tables
wide-open bibles
on the bedroom floor
cutting down souls

believer
the cross around your thick neck
said so
pleasure not
a word in your sermon
when you stood behind
the pulpit

into temptation

I've never seen
my wife naked, you said
that afternoon
as you washed my body
of your milky venom

tiny, were your feet, short
were your legs, hanging
from your round belly
searching
in the dark of night
in my bed

I am sorry
you said
in the break of day

after you fired the torches
on the wood deck,
broke glass

no gin left
while I hid behind the covers
by the Blue Ridge Mountains

flames
burned
down
home
ignited
sin

hell

no lullaby
can awaken
you

tiny.

Ana Martínez Orizondo (AMO) is a Cuban born visual artist, poet and Emmy award-winning television producer living in Coral Gables, Florida. Her writing has appeared in Blue Mountain Review, Newtown Literary, and The Journal of Latina Critical Feminism to name a few.

As a visual artist, Ana has exhibited in group shows in Miami, New York and online. She collaborated with fashion designer, Gabriela Hearst on her Fall Winter 2022 collection and was the inaugural artist-in-residence at The Chequit, Shelter Island with a solo show from her Tree Stories series.

Her artwork resides in private collections and has been featured nationally and internationally in *Vogue Mexico & Latin America, Orion Magazine, The Cut, Cottages & Gardens, Shelter Island Reporter, Art Seen Magazine,* and *The Hopper Magazine* among others.

She holds an MA in Liberal Arts from Florida International University and a BA in Latin American Literature and Communications from the University of Pennsylvania.

Milton Keynes UK
Ingram Content Group UK Ltd.
UKHW010006260624
444693UK00003B/43

9 798888 386071